Second-hand Abuse

The Power and Control Personality
(And Their Victims)

By
S. F. Bellsmith

PublishAmerica
Baltimore

First printing

ISBN: 1-4137-4686-1
PUBLISHED BY PUBLISHAMERICA, LLLP
www.publishamerica.com
Baltimore

Printed in the United States of America

Acknowledgments

First, I want to thank my husband and children for their support and encouragement. Their belief in me saw me through many dreary, tedious days of this project.

Secondly, I want to thank the many clients who shared their, at times heart wrenching, stories with me. Thank you for your trust and for the privilege of helping sort through, or "pull apart," your issues to expose the lies believed and replace them with truth so you could make more informed choices that would affect the balance of your lives. You truly are to be applauded!

Thirdly, I want to thank Carman Wilson (who wrote the foreword for this book) for his years of consultation. Painstakingly you helped me "pull apart" issues presented in the counselling room. Thank you for persevering and making me look at myself with brutal honesty, so that I could better help my clients.

Fourthly, I want to thank Christopher John Corsini for taking my scribbles and letting his magical fingers run over the computer keyboard to create the illustrations throughout this book.

Fifthly, I want to thank my home church, Stanley Avenue Baptist, in Hamilton, Ontario, for being brave enough to allow me to open the counselling arm of ministry. Together, we have seen this center grow and become well-established in our community and beyond. Because of the church's faith and support, I have grown personally, spiritually, and as a counsellor. Thank you!

Sixthly, I want to thank my friends and prayer partners who have played such an important role in keeping me on track and encouraged me to keep ploughing ahead. You truly are precious gifts from our loving Heavenly Father. Thank you!

Transcending all is my profound thanks to the One who has made it all possible: My Father, God. His gifting, preparation, encouragement, and presence is beyond imagination and could easily fill another book.

Contents

Disclaimer

The material presented in this book comes from the experiences of more than one hundred clients over a six-year period. All names are fictional.

One mini case study represents a couple where the male is the power and control personality and the female is the victim mentality. The other mini case study represents a couple where the female is the power and control personality and the male is the victim mentality.

All information is a collective and does not reflect any one individual or couple.

This is not a scientific study, but the well-founded opinion of the author and counsellor.

Foreword

When Sietske Bellsmith first asked me to edit the initial manuscript of her book, I was pleased. I had had the pleasure of supervising Ms. Bellsmith in her counselling practice and I knew the caliber of her work. As the manuscript developed, I was impressed with what was evolving and I was honored when she asked me to write this foreword.

Ms. Bellsmith has presented us with an insightful study that illuminates the impact of the power and control personality on the dynamics of the marital relationship. This is a much needed study, not only from the power and control perspective, but also from the perspective of the victim. It brings to the reader's attention the nature of the unconscious power that the victim possesses.

Without in any way identifying the people involved, Ms. Bellsmith has drawn on her experience with couples with whom she has worked in her clinical practice. The end result is a very practical guide for marriage counsellors who work with power and control personalities and their victims in marital relationships.

D. Carman Wilson M.A.; MEd.; M. Div.; C.C.H.

Introduction

The idea for this book was born primarily because there seemed to be so little material devoted to the crippling effects of power and control in the lives of so many of the clients coming through my doors.

Over the years, I found myself recreating *The Power and Control Wheel,* as well as creating other exercises I constantly used with clients. While using these exercises, often a client would look perplexed and say, "I didn't know you knew my husband/wife/partner/parents," etc., when I had never met the person they were referring to. To me this indicated the accuracy of these exercises.

The Power and Control Wheel that you will find in this book was redeveloped from the wheel put out by "Domestic Abuse Intervention Project," of Duluth, Minnesota. The revamped *Power and Control Wheel* takes you through a chronological journey that seems to be characteristic of many power and control personalities.

Together, through these pages, we will look at what constitutes abuse, the power and control personality, the victim mentality, and equality in relationships

You will get a rare glimpse of the power and control personality and the victim mentality from behind closed doors as you meet Liz & Brad and James & Amy. It is hoped that you will see the significant role power and control has played in their lives. I will track for you their backgrounds, as well as their common traits.

I will lead you along the path these couples traveled in an effort to enable you to experience life with a power and control personality. As I do this, you will be able to see how the tools referred to in *The Power and Control Wheel* were used in their day-to-day lives.

Towards the close of this book, I will look at ways to reverse the victim mentality that is so much a part of people caught up in power and control, as well as the power and control personality.

Chapter 1
What is abuse?

Abuse is a confusing word for most people. According to the American Heritage Dictionary, abuse is: 1. "To use wrongly or improperly; misuse: abuse alcohol; abuse a privilege. 2. To hurt or injure by maltreatment; ill-use. 3. To force sexual activity on; rape or molest. 4. To assail with contemptuous, coarse, or insulting words; revile."

According to the above definition, most of us have been abused at sometime in our lives. All of the forms of abuse mentioned tend to bring anger into the core part of our being. Let's break that down, or using one of my favorite phrases, let's "pull it apart."

By far the most frequent issue presented in the counselling room is **Anger**.

Anger: Turned inside or unresolved, ferments and often develops into **Depression**.

Depression: Often turns to severe **Insecurity**.

Insecurity: Often turns to the silent need for **Self-Promotion**.

Self-promotion: Often turns to the need to choose a **Victim**. Someone to have power over and control of; someone to push down so self can be raised up.

Power and Control: Often leads to **Abuse**. Abuse in verbal, mental, emotional, physical and/or sexual forms. All forms of abuse lead to the destruction of the person victimized.

Abuse: Causes deep wounds that often determine what direction life will take. For this study, we will look at those who choose to develop **The Power and Control Personality** and those who choose to develop the **Victim Mentality.**

It seems that we still live in a society that says, "If there aren't any bruises, you haven't been abused." Someone who didn't constantly have names hurled at them must have written the old adage "Sticks and stones may break my bones, but names will never hurt me." Anyone who has lived under a barrage of horribly insulting names knows how hurtful they can be! These wounds only become visible if a hand, foot, or fist have accompanied the application process of these names. As hard and embarrassing as a physical wound can be, it really is only skin deep. The degradation of the name-calling, as well as the rest of the tools used by the power and control personality, drill right into the core part of the human soul. They have the ability to turn a person into a victim, especially when the person to whom these names are being directed already suffers from low self-esteem. That is when the names are heard in a manner that perpetuates low self-esteem.

Children growing up in this atmosphere may not be the initial targets of verbal, physical, or sexual abuse, but that doesn't mean they aren't being abused. The way a small child processes information is very matter of fact. For instance, if a boy constantly hears his mother being called a bitch, among other things, his thought process maybe something like this: My mother is female, my father is male, my father seems to hate my mother and calls her all these horrible things, therefore females aren't worth much. As this boy grows up, he too will treat women in the way demonstrated to him. If it's a girl growing up in the same type of household, her thought process maybe something like this: My mother is female, my father is male, my father seems to hate my mother and calls her all these horrible things. I am female, therefore I'm not worth very much. As she grows up, she may expect to be treated in the same way as her mother, thinking that as normal.

Thus, the cycle continues!

We could recount hundreds, if not thousands, of similar situations, but that will have to wait for another book.

Children are often the victims of second-hand abuse. Second-hand abuse can be just as deadly, if not more so, because as these children grow up, they often either lash out and abuse or continue to be victimized. The only emotion they learned to handle (and that with a great deal of distortion) was anger. In their minds, anger supersedes all other emotions, leaving them feeling confused and very insecure about their world. As a result, many develop the power and control personality in an attempt to hide their insecurities and revert back to a familiar outlet for their anger. Others grow up, developing the victim mentality and continue to be used, abused, and often thrown away. The same deep-rooted insecurities are at the core of both personality types.

In order for children to grow up feeling secure, they need to be given consistent boundaries that provides them with the safety to explore their logical world as well as their feelings. I use the playpen illustration (described later in this chapter) in sessions when working with parents or families.

Not only do children need to have boundaries, they need to understand the purpose of such boundaries. When the child is an infant, the parent(s) might choose to use a playpen. Using this boundary technique, several things happen. First, the parent(s) are assured the child is safe and has everything they need. Second, the child can see the parent(s), therefore develops the feeling that they belong. Third, the child learns to explore its world in safety, yet is able to observe outside their walls. Fourth, the child feels safe and develops a sense of security, and a high level of self-esteem begins to be built. Fifth, consistency is being witnessed and learned.

As the infant grows into a toddler, the playpen might become the enclosed front porch. As a preschooler, the playpen might be the fenced-in backyard. After that, the boundary might be to the corner and back, then around the block, then to school and back. At first, the boundaries are visible, but as the child grows, they quickly become invisible boundaries. At each stage, the child needs to develop feelings of safety, security, connection with family, as well as the sense of adventure that comes with permission to explore their world in their own way within the boundaries they have experienced.

If the infant or toddler had the power of speech, they might say something like this: "Love me enough to let me know I really really matter to you." They might also say, "Let me feel secure enough in your love for me by limiting my world to a manageable size so I won't feel too scared."

Unfortunately, the child growing up in the power and control environment has not been given consistently safe boundaries. This often results in insecurity about their parents, their feelings, themselves, as well as confusion about the world around them.

If the child develops the victim mentality, it will affect every aspect of life. It dictates their belief system, their intellect, their decision-making process, their self-esteem, even their very identity. The victim mentality will be constantly second-guessing themselves and wondering why they can never get anything accomplished. The power and control partner will have them truly believing that if only they tried harder to please him/her, life would be fine, thus placing the responsibility of the success or failure of the relationship squarely on the victim's shoulders.

In the succeeding chapters we will see the tools the power and control personality uses, as well as the distorted rules and/ or beliefs the victim mentality uses. Later on, we will look at ways to break the cycle of abuse by reversing both the power and control personality, as well as the victim mentality.

Chapter 2
The Power and Control Personality

In the previous chapter, we briefly saw how the power and control personality, as well as the victim mentality, were created.

The vast majority of power and control personalities grew up in a household where one or both parents were extremely controlling, making it a learned behavior. In this atmosphere, the child would often see raw anger turn into rage. It would be common for them to hide under the bed or in a closet to avoid hearing the verbal attack from one parent against the other, as well as to stay out of reach of the out of control angry parent who would be likely to strike out. They come face-to-face with the unfairness of this rage, invariably not understanding what started it and not daring to ask. As children grow up in this setting, they often internalize their intense emotions and invariably develop a false belief that somehow all the chaos and dysfunction is their fault. They grow up in a constant state of fear with no consistency that tells them, "If I do this or that, then mom/dad will be angry with me." They grow up in a constant state of not knowing what will set mom/dad off or what the severity of the attack will be this time. This produces a great deal of insecurity within the child. A high level of guilt evolves, (if only I try harder) believing that somehow they are to blame for the outbursts that will augment their insecurities.

In this type of dysfunctional family, there is no one to teach the child how to deal with his/her insecurities. As these insecurities intensify, the child will either withdraw and develop the victim mentality, or will lash out in the same way demonstrated by mom or dad, which begins the development of the power and control personality. By choosing this route, the child doesn't have to deal with their own insecurities. Their insecurities either become an open book for others to exploit (victim mentality), or something to work hard at hiding from the world around them (the power and control personality). As long as the power and control personality can hide behind their insecurities, they have a false sense that they don't have to deal with the wounds that created the insecurities in the first place.

The power and control personality develops a belief system that basically convinces him/her that "I really do know the 'right' way to do pretty much everything." As long as he/she can hang on to that superior belief, he/she won't be forced to take a look at all his/her own insecurities. It's almost like he/she has built an invisible wall around these insecurities to keep everyone from seeing the mess.

The building of this wall absorbs a great deal of energy. They will invariably develop new strategies as each layer of the wall is constructed. Strategies like 1) A swagger in their walk, trying to indicate that they haven't got a care in the world. 2) A smooth tongue that has a way of convincing most neighbors and peers that they are wonderful, upstanding members of society. Most power and control personalities would make great con artists. 3) A honing device that is able to almost instantly find a victim mentality in virtually any setting. There may be one hundred people present with only one victim mentality among them, but the power and control personality will quickly zero in and spot the victim. 4) Attentive, listening ears that gives the impression that they really care.

Once the power and control personality has zeroed in and found a possible victim, he/she begins the dance of winning their confidence. The power and control personality systematically uses the above strategies to try and convince the victim mentality that they have found a safe haven. The following power and control wheel takes us through a chronological journey that many power and control personalities seem to use.

The Power and Control Wheel*

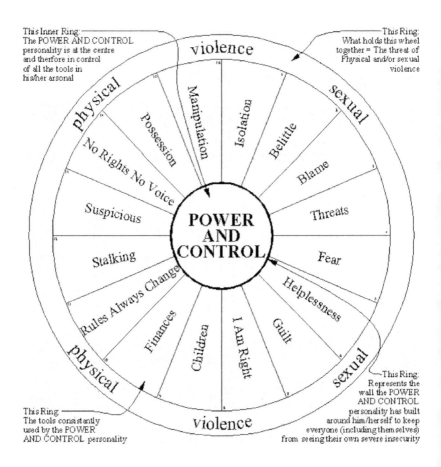

The Power and Control Wheel was redeveloped from the wheel put out by "Domestic Abuse Intervention Project," of Duluth, Minnesota.

Tools the Power and Control Personality Systematically Uses

Isolation:

When a partner choice has been made (here after referred to as victim), the power and control personality subtly pulls their victim away from friends and family. Phrases like: "They don't really like me," or "Your friends don't understand me," or "I just want us to spend all our time together" are often used.

At this stage the victim gets in touch with their paternal/maternal instinct and will try to comfort, support, and please. They might even be flattered that this wonderful person has chosen them, so they had better not blow it.

The reason the victim is pulled away from friends and family is because everybody connected to the victim is seen as a threat by the power and control personality. The power and control personality lives in great fear that someone will see him/her for who they really are and disclose this to their chosen victim.

Slowly, the victim's world begins to shrink. The victim finds themselves making excuses not to attend family functions or to go out with friends to events that have always been important before.

During the dating period, the power and control personality uses a less threatening approach. Once the victim find themselves committed to the relationship, the power and control personality tends to use much stronger, even threatening tactics.

Belittling:

During the dating period, the belittling is also very subtle. Remember, the power and control personality has to push someone else down in order to feel superior to at least one person in this world. At first, phrases like, "You're not really going to wear that are you?" or "Another bowl of ice cream, you think that's wise?" Using these types of phrases, the power and control personality has very subtly told the victim that: 1) they have no sense of style, 2) they need someone else to tell them what is appropriate, 3) they are not very smart, 4) they are an embarrassment, 5) they had better not get fat, 6) they had better check with their partner on virtually everything.

Once a commitment to the relationship has been made, the belittling is increased. Very quickly the victim is told they are a good for nothing, stupid, fat slob. (And I've been very kind with my choice of words).

Blame:

The power and control personality finds it virtually impossible to blame themselves. As a result, everything negative that happens is: a) their victim's fault, b) society's fault, c) their parents' fault, d) the bosses' fault, e) the bank's fault, f) the neighbor's fault. Well, you get the idea. If the power and control personality were to start taking personal responsibility, they would need to begin breaking down that wall they took such pains to build around themselves in the first place. As long as they can deflect the blame, they can continue to hide behind the wall of insecurities and live in their pretend world. If at all possible, they like to blame their chosen victim, as it gives them yet another reason to belittle.

Threats:

The power and control personality often uses threats or threatening gestures and follows through on enough of them to instill fear into their victim. The victim will quickly develop a belief that unless they are extremely careful and obedient, the threats uttered will most definitely come true. At the beginning, there maybe threatening gestures, such as hitting their fist in their hand or pounding the wall right beside the victim's head or towering over top of the victim to make them feel small. Sometimes the threat is offering a reward, such as a night out, and then revoking it. If the victim mentality begins to stand up for themselves, the threats usually become much more vicious. Threats like: a) "If you even think of leaving me, I'll kill you;" or, "If you leave me, no court in this land would ever give a terrible mother/father like you custody of the children. I'd take them away and you would never see them again;" or, "If you leave me, I'll kill myself."

Fear:

One of the ways the power and control personality makes themselves believe they are superior to their chosen victim is to instill fear on an ongoing basis. The victim will experience knots of anxiety in the pit of their stomach when approaching their home, not knowing if they will be in trouble once they enter. Or the victim will scurry around the house straightening or cleaning anything the power and control personality has ever screamed at them for, beaten them for, belittled them for, etc. They never know what will set their partner off; thus they live with an almost constant knot in their stomach. This becomes a way of life, and before long they believe this too is normal.

Helplessness:

If the victim begins to fight back and insists they aren't going to put up with their partner's behavior anymore, the power and control personality may revert to the helpless child tactic. They will plead for their victim to help them become a "better person," that they will "try harder," and that they are so sorry about "it" (usually physical abuse) and "it" will never happen again. "Please give me another chance." This tactic hooks the maternal/paternal part of their victim, who will want to come to the power and control personality's rescue. Usually, as soon as the victim is back in their place, everything returns to what the power and control personality deems normal.

Remember, the power and control personality needs a victim so they can keep believing they are superior to at least this one person. As long as this belief stays in place, they don't have to look at their own insecurities.

Guilt:

The power and control personality becomes an expert in heaping guilt on to their victim. It often goes along with the "helpless me" tool. The power and control personality actually has the ability to make the victim mentality feel guilty at not being good enough for them, for not being a good enough lover, for not being smart enough, for not being grateful that their partner chose them, for not being thankful that their partner is willing to teach them how to do everything the "right" way, etc.

This is often another form of blaming, belittling, and threatening, but done in such a way the victim mentality experiences a deep sense of guilt. For what?—they often can't explain.

A low level of self-esteem + fear = guilt.

"I Am Right":

To guard the wall that protects their insecurities, the power and control personality MUST be right about pretty much everything! With the victim so beaten down and belittled, they are easily programmed to believe anything their partner tells them. The power and control personality makes the victim believe theirs is the only right way to: a) wash the dishes, b) set the table, c) drive the car, d) discipline the kids, e) fry an egg, f) sweep the floor. Well, the list could go on and on, but you get the idea, right? The victim soon realizes that they must learn to do everything the "right way" or constantly be in trouble. As a result, the victim's sense that they can do nothing right and that there must be something wrong with them is reinforced.

Children:

The power and control personality will use whatever is necessary in order to maintain their controlling position. This includes using their own children. If the victim start to stand up for him/herself, the children often become the targets. The victim instinctively will suffer to try to keep their children safe.

Finances:

The power and control personalities will either hold all the family finances so the victim has to beg for anything they need, or will hand all the financial responsibilities to the victim. This is done so that when (and there will be a when) things go wrong they will have another reason to blame, belittle, threaten, and instill fear into their victim.

Rules Always Change:

The power and control personality needs to keep everyone (especially his/her victim) guessing. As a result, they will continually change the rules, i.e. today it is okay to leave the dishes in the sink until tomorrow, but if a glass is left in the sink a few days later, it could easily bring, "You don't ever do anything around here. You're nothing but a lazy good for nothing b__ "

Depending on the mood of the power control personality, violence often accompanies this lack of respect for their rules; rules that the victim can only guess at because they are never spelled out. The victim lives in constant fear, hoping their actions and/or behavior won't cause an avalanche of abuse from their partner.

Stalking:

The power and control personality must know where their victim is at all times. They might not necessarily follow them (although that is not uncommon), but if the victim is expected to be at a certain place at a certain time, they will phone, and if the phone isn't picked up, the power and control personality goes crazy and often accusations of affairs and/or violence follows.

Suspicious:

Due to the power and control personality's own insecurities, they constantly suspect their partner of cheating on them. They are so afraid that their victim will finally see them for who they really are and find someone else to love. That is why the stalking tool is so important in their own eyes.

The power and control personality might even bug the phone or scroll through to see who has called their partner while they were out. They might even call these numbers and demand to know what the caller had wanted.

No Rights, No Voice:

Through the use of all these tools, the victim continuously loses more and more of their own identity. They cease to eat the foods they like because their partner says they are disgusting. They cease to wear the colors and styles they like because their partner doesn't like them. From their hairstyle to the way they dust the furniture, and pretty much everything in between, the victim ceases to be their own person and feels more and more like a possession.

Manipulation:

The power and control personality has become very skilled at manipulation. That is, to get their victim to do what they want, how they want, when they want, and where they want, knowing full well that the victim doesn't want to do it in the first place. They often are able to convince their victim (as well as themselves) that certain events were as they remember them, when in reality they often were completely opposite.

If the victim defends him/herself and takes a stand against the wishes or demands of the power and control personality, a number of possibilities often happen. a) The power and control personality may "accidentally" destroy something that is especially precious to the victim (i.e. a pet or a family treasure). b) The power and control personality will use threats, intimidation, insults, or bullying to get what they want. In other words, instill a higher than normal voltage of fear into the victim. c) The power and control personality may simply start hitting out of fear of losing the position of superiority.

Not all power and control personalities need to use all of the above tools at all times. As long as the victim allows him/herself to be treated in a derogatory manner that diminishes who they are and magnifies the superiority of their partner, everything runs relatively peacefully.

If the victim begins to fight back and refuses to be conned by their partner any longer, that's when the power and control personality will invariably pull out all stops and use whatever tools he/she deems necessary to maintain their position.

What holds the power and control wheel together, and usually keeps the victim mentality in check, is the very real threat of physical or sexual violence.

Chapter 3
The Victim Mentality

Distorted Rules and/or Beliefs of the Victim Mentality:

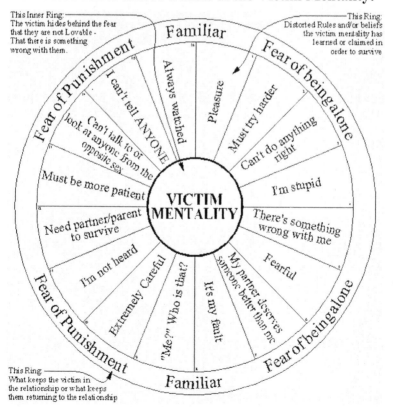

This Inner Ring:
The victim hides behind the fear that they are not Lovable - That there is something wrong with them.

This Ring:
Distorted Rules and/or beliefs the victim mentality has learned or claimed in order to survive

This Ring:
What keeps the victim in the relationship or what keeps them returning to the relationship

Familiar

Fear of Punishment

Fear of being alone

Always watched

Pleasure

Must try harder

Can't do anything right

I can't tell ANYONE

Can't talk to or look at anyone from the opposite sex

I'm stupid

Must be more patient

VICTIM MENTALITY

There's something wrong with me

Need partner/parent to survive

Fearful

I'm not heard

My partner deserves someone better than me

Extremely Careful

"Me?" Who is that?

It's my fault

Fear of Punishment

Fear of being alone

Familiar

The victim mentality wheel was created after years of observation and listening to the victims who lived with power and control personalities.

I entitled this wheel "Distorted Rules and/or Beliefs." This was done because these rules or beliefs have not been formed due to the victim mentality's own sense of self. They have been formed primarily from input the controlling individual(s) planted in their lives. The victim mentality has a sense of constantly being detached from their own thoughts, feelings, and sense of worth, and are always trying to grab on to what they believe their partner might be asking of them. The victim mentality always seems to be floundering, and is never sure of what is expected of them.

The following are "distorted" primarily because they are based on lies that the victim mentality believes to be true. The power and control personality needs their victim to believe these lies because the energy that is needed to try and fulfill these rules or maintain these beliefs keeps the victim from finding their own inner strength. The power and control personality knows that if the victim were to find, and begin to use, their own inner strength, they would very quickly see through the tactics used by the power and control personality in their lives and fight back.

Not all power and control personalities necessarily have to use all the tools on the power and control wheel, neither do all victim mentalities adhere to all of these rules and/or beliefs. However, each of the victim mentalities that I have seen over the years has displayed many of these distorted rules and beliefs. Let's have a look at what they mean.

Pleaser:

The victim mentality develops the pleaser mentality theory early on in life. The main premise for that is the hope that if they can foresee what the power and control personality in their lives needs or wants, then if they can fulfill those needs, hopefully they will forestall any angry outbursts that would be aimed directly at them.

The victim mentality seldom gives themselves permission to consider their own wishes or needs. They are constantly trying to foresee everyone else's wishes, especially that of the power and control personality in their lives. By this method they hope to keep the opportunities for anger, rage, and/or violence to a minimum.

Must Try Harder:

Along with the pleaser trait, the victim mentality has been convinced (usually by the power and control personality in their lives) that everything in their relationship, finances, etc. would be just fine if they only tried harder. As a result, the victim mentality carries the full weight of failure or success on their shoulders.

Anything the power and control personality sees as going wrong, or things that have brought verbal and/or physical abuse in the past, brings the victim mentality face to face with the fact that they must do better—try harder—to learn how to do everything the "correct" way. Then and only then is it possible for peace to reign.

However, the victim mentality is seldom given a hint as to when he/she has tried hard enough to be able to relax a little.

Seldom is praise or affirmation given for trying so hard. All the victim mentality hears is what was not right—only the negatives are brought out for examination.

Can't Do Anything Right:

Following close on the heels of the pleaser and must try harder is the belief that they (the victim mentality) can't do anything "right."

When a child grows up in a household with a power and control personality, they have learned how to please, how to try harder, and even how everything should be done according to the power and control parent's wishes.

When this child marries, he/she has a sense of confidence that they know how to please, how to try harder, and how to do things "right." The problem is their mate is different! Their mate seems to have their own idea of how everything should be done and they aren't willing to put up with any other way.

Now the victim mentality has to learn all over again. He/she wants to please, wants to try hard, but doesn't seem to be able to do anything in the new "right" way.

The result is a sudden plunge of their self-esteem, which gets fed by the belittling, blaming, etc. the power and control personality uses regularly.

I'm Stupid:

The victim mentality quickly comes to the conclusion that he/she must be stupid. With each task that has to be relearned the "right" way—to avoid trouble—a small piece of their sense of worth or intellect is chipped away and is sucked into a vacuum.

The fact that the power and control personality continually

helps to reinforce the sense of stupidity in the victim mentality (see Power and Control Wheel in chapter two) only cements the idea as fact. This takes him/her to the next belief on the victim mentality wheel.

There's Something Wrong with Me:

During all of the above rules or beliefs, the victim mentality is in constant conflict. His/her logic says one thing, but when feelings come, they seem to say something totally different.

Along with the inner conflict is the fact that all through his/her growing up years, they were never given permission to discover who they were. Or how they would do something, given the choice. Or what their opinion or thought was on any given subject. All their lives have had to be centered on someone else—the power and control personality in their lives.

This left huge vacancies in their own personalities, their own creativity, their own intellect, their own sense of worth, and their own dignity.

No wonder I hear so often in the counselling room, "There is something wrong with me!" The saddest part is, they truly believe it.

Fearful:

Keeping in mind the tools the power and control personality uses, as well as the above beliefs the victim mentality has laid claim to, no wonder the victim mentality develops this intense fear that is constantly in the forefront.

This fear seems to sit in the pit of their stomach and gnaws away at any pretense of peace. It makes the victim mentality almost panicky when approaching home after work or grocery shopping. It makes the victim mentality scurry around the house the last half hour or so, prior to the expected arrival of the power and control personality, to straighten shoes, wash dishes, set the table, make sure beds are made, make sure clothes are picked up, etc.

The victim mentality will pull out the mental file that is marked "This doesn't please me," which is jam-packed with everything he/she has ever been yelled at or struck for. With the file figuratively in hand, they run through the house checking to make sure the power and control personality won't have anything to be angry about. The victim mentality soon realizes that if the power and control personality has had one of "those" days, it doesn't matter that all seems to be in perfect order, they will find something to become angry about and will make sure that the victim pays for it in some way.

My Partner Deserves Someone Better Than Me:

With the belief that he/she isn't worth much, the victim mentality truly believes they are a great burden to their mate. They are not aware that that is exactly what the power and control personality in their lives has worked so hard to make them feel. The power and control personality will reinforce this sense that the victim isn't worthy of them by saying things like, "Who would ever put up with you?" or "You sure are lucky I'm such a patient man/woman;" or "Who would ever hire you, you can't even…"

All of this only makes the victim mentality try harder to please.

It's My Fault:

The victim mentality can try their hardest to please and keep trying to learn how to do everything in their mate's way, but it still won't be enough.

The power and control personality has an incredible ability to focus blame for almost anything, and their favorite target is the victim mentality they have chosen to live with. For example, an angry power and control personality had his hands around his wife's throat, choking the life out of her. When he finally let go, she dropped to the floor. He loomed over her in a rage and spewed, "Look what you made me do!"

Through the above type of logic, the victim mentality becomes convinced that "it" must be their fault. Whatever "it" is! The victim mentality goes back to their belief that there's something wrong with them and that they're not very smart, therefore they must try harder to please and understand. Yet there is also the sense that they really don't know what they have done to create such rage in their partner. Confusion reigns!

Me? Who Is That?:

The victim mentality honestly gets bewildered if someone asks them who they are. I know, as I see it in their faces so many times in the counselling room. It's almost like the question, which gives them permission to actually think about themselves, is too foreign for their thought process.

All their lives they have existed to meet someone else's needs and expectations, primarily whoever was the power and control personality in their lives at the time. Never have they been encouraged to find out who they are as individuals in their own rights.

Extremely Careful:

The victim mentality learns to be extremely careful regarding: who they talk to, who they look at, what they wear, what they eat, where to keep private notes or a journal, how to make suggestions, how or where to get help, who to confide in. No doubt, if you identify yourself, a friend, or loved one in these pages, you can add many more to this list.

If the victim mentality has children living in the home, they will deflect all the abuse on to themselves, away from the children. Often it's not until the victim mentality sees his/her children being abused that they will start to formulate a plan of escape. Their theory seems to be, "You can treat me like shit, but don't you dare touch my children." After all, a large part of the victim mentality believes they deserve to be treated in this manner. It is familiar!

I'm Not Heard:

With the constant whittling away of the victim mentality's self-esteem and intellect, the victim mentality ceases to have any voice at all. This is reinforced by the power and control personality who continually belittles them whenever they dare to give an opinion. This even happens if the power and control personality asks for their opinion. If the power and control personality appears to actually ask the victim for their opinion, the victim quickly assesses what they believe their partner wants to hear and feeds this to them. They know that their honest opinion is most likely only going to get trampled on anyway, so they find ways to guard their own thoughts.

It doesn't take children in the home long before they too treat the victim mentality in the manner as demonstrated by the control personality parent. This seems to be especially true with same-sex children to the power and control personality.

Need Partner/Parent to Survive:

It's like the victim mentality has been programmed to believe that they would not survive life without a power and control personality in charge.

When you look at all the previous rules or beliefs, it is easy to understand where this belief came from. This is especially true when you compare it to the tools the power and control personality uses in the previous chapter.

Must Be More Patient:

The victim mentality becomes so used to blaming themselves, as well as the uncertainty of their partner' s reactions, that they constantly admonish themselves to be more patient. Don't forget, the full weight of whether or not their relationship with their partner will succeed or fail has been purposely placed on their shoulders. The victim mentality, having been programmed to believe they are stupid and can't do anything right, finds themselves in constant conflict. An inner war rages! Their logic seems to tell them one thing, yet their emotions keep pulling them back into the same disheveled mess that they can't seem to get out of. This dovetails nicely with the need to please and to try harder. That's when the belief that if they can only learn to be more patient is born.

Can't Talk to (or Look at) Anyone from the Opposite Sex:

At the beginning of the relationship, the victim mentality actually thought their partner's seeming jealousy was cute. He/she chose to believe that their partner's dislike of anyone of the opposite sex, looking and/or speaking to them, was a sign of how much the power control personality loved them. For a period of time the victim mentality can make themselves believe that it is their partner's cute insecurities that makes them so unreasonable in this area.

Not long after a commitment to the relationship has been made does the victim mentality begin to realize that they will never be able to innocently speak to or even glance at anyone from the opposite sex, ever again! The victim mentality soon realizes that this is one area he/she has to be most extremely careful as this is the number one reason for their partner to go into a rage and/or often become violent. As a result, the victim mentality cuts him/herself off from all friends of the opposite sex or becomes extremely sneaky about these friendships.

I Can't Tell Anyone:

Not long after a commitment to the relationship the victim mentality begins to feel trapped. Their partner continually isolates them from their known world. They feel stupid and totally unsure of who they are or what they want. Then there's the constant strain that everything negative is their fault. The heaviness wears on them to the point that a deep sadness settles into the core part of their being.

The victim mentality begins to ask themselves questions like: "Is this what it's supposed to be like, being in a relationship?" "Maybe I really do deserve this kind of treatment?" "Would anyone believe me?" "If I tell, will my life be worth living?" "Could I make it without him/her always telling me what to do or think or believe?" "Would he/she really harm me or my children if I told?" "Is there such a thing as a 'safe' place where I can go?"

The deeper the questions, the sadder the victim mentality becomes. The sadder they become, the more trapped they feel. The more trapped they feel, the more they blame themselves. The more they blame themselves, the angrier they become. The angrier they become, the more likely they are to take the "risk" in telling someone.

Telling someone is the first step to freedom. However, this process could literally take years as the victim mentality weighs the pros and cons over and over and over. Don't forget, a great deal of fear has been instilled. Along with the fear, a sense of deep shame is also present.

Always Watched:

The victim mentality often looks over their shoulders expecting to see someone watching them. This is especially true when the victim mentality becomes disillusioned with their partner and starts making plans to escape. They are very aware of their partner's suspicious nature and how he/she will use friends to spy on them.

The victim mentality will seldom meet a friend at the same location as their last meeting. They will take different routes to and from work. They will use pay phones, rather than the phone from either work or home.

It's almost like the more the power and control personality makes the victim feel stupid, the smarter the victim becomes.

For the victim to set his/her course towards freedom and self-awareness often takes an incredible amount of courage and planning.

If the victim hopes to be able to cease being the victim within the relationship, he/she often needs to change gradually. This is difficult if the power and control personality hasn't come to the realization that change is necessary or if change isn't what they want. The power and control personality may simply continue to apply more and more pressure on the victim mentality who is struggling to find a way to stop being the victim.

If the victim mentality realizes that to stay in the relationship will mean that their only choice is to remain a victim, they may want to start planning to enter a safe shelter. If this needs to be the choice for the victim, extreme care has to be given to the method of separation.

Sometimes, it's when the victim finally leaves that the power and control personality is shaken into the need to start looking at themselves and what changes they may need to make in order not to lose their partner. This is often when a power and control personality will finally admit to needing help and seek counselling.

Sometimes, when the victim is in the planning stage of his/her escape, they are in the greatest danger from their power and control partner. This is often when the power and control personality resorts to the use of physical and/or sexual violence.

It is important for the victim to build a support group who will step in at a moment's notice to help move the victim to a safe shelter.

If the victim is dealing with a full-blown power and control partner (someone who consistently uses the vast majority of the tools on the power and control wheel), police intervention might be necessary. Anyone who helps in the planning or escape may also become a target for revenge.

Be careful, be smart, and be safe!

Chapter 4
Common Traits and Backgrounds

Let me introduce you to our sample couples and give you a glimpse into their history.

First we have Brad and Liz.

Brad's parents divorced when he was in his early teens. Prior to the separation and ultimate divorce, his father was extremely abusive and controlling. Brad grew up never knowing what would set his father off or who would be at the receiving end of his violent abuse. Brad would often be awakened in the middle of the night by the screaming attacks in his parent's bedroom. Brad remembers trying to cover his ears with pillows to stop from hearing, but it was hard to hear his mother called extremely derogatory names. He also knew that soon he would hear his dad beating on his mom.

Being a small child, Brad often felt helpless and could tell you about all the possible hiding places in his entire house.

As Brad grew and decided he was strong enough, he would often try to come to his mother's defense. This, of course, put him in the direct line of fire. Brad's body is scarred from the abuse he took trying to protect his mother and younger siblings.

Entering his teen years, Brad started to hear his father's

words come from his own mouth, especially when they were directed at his mother. The frightened child, who desperately tried to shield his mother from his father's violence, seemed to experience a complete metamorphosis. It was as if Brad made himself analyze his father's role, his mother's role (which also became his as he defended her more and more), and determined in the innermost part of his being that no one was ever going to be able to use him as a punching bag ever again. Drawing from his only other experience, the logical choice for him was to become the aggressor in order to stop being the victim.

The scary part is, he most likely wasn't even aware of his inner resolve. He just started acting on it.

By his late teens, Brad had become the very person he had fought against all his life. He had become his father—a full-blown power and control personality.

During Brad's late teens, he became very conscious and protective of what he let others see about him. He always spoke appropriately and even with respect to his peers and neighbors. His dress was immaculate and he appeared to be a well-adjusted student. For the most part, he was liked and highly thought of.

However, behind closed doors, he terrorized his mother and siblings until he was finally told to leave the house. Brad tried living with his father for a while, but soon discovered that the only role open to him in his father's house was that of victim.

Brad found himself trying to survive while living on an emotional roller coaster. He was determined never to be victimized again, so he would often become the aggressor, even with his father. However, his father would shout something or make a familiar gesture towards him, and Brad would revert back to being a small, frightened little boy. Not only did Brad find this emotional flip-flop experience maddening, it was also exhausting. It wasn't long before he realized that he could no longer live in his father's house.

Forced to live on his own, Brad soon began to hang around with the party crowd. His new "friends" persuaded him to experiment with drugs and alcohol, and it didn't take long before his alcohol consumption was way in excess.

What would appear to have been a sheer act of the will, Brad managed to hold down a part-time job, finish school, and still be an active participant in this party lifestyle. The amazing part is that he managed to keep this all going for nearly twelve years.

At a party thrown for Brad's 30th birthday, he met Liz.

Liz is the oldest child. She has two sisters and two brothers. Both of Liz's parents are alcoholics, although they would never use that word themselves.

Liz was a high needs child, as she was often sick and suffered from several severe allergies. As a result, she was often made to feel as if she was a real bother to have around, especially by her own mother. During one of her attacks, Liz talked about being afraid to go to her parents for help, as she hated the heavy sighs and belittling comments she was sure to get from them. She was constantly reminded that none of her sisters or brothers were as much of a nuisance as she was.

When both parents drank heavily, they became very abusive, and as the oldest, Liz often got the worst of the violent attacks.

By the time Liz reached the age of nine or ten, she started sneaking out of the house to hide from her parents' attacks. Liz and her brother, who was one and a half years younger, would often sneak food from the kitchen and start corralling the younger ones out to one of their hiding places. Their parents' drinking usually started around four in the afternoon, so whatever food the older two managed to sneak out often became supper for the group. Liz's brother would sneak back to the house to see if their parents had passed out yet. If they hadn't, it meant waiting and hiding. If they had, it meant creeping back inside past the snoring, drooling hulks lying wherever they dropped, and putting the younger children to bed. Then Liz and her brother would start the long, tedious, and often dangerous, job of getting their parents into their beds.

Even though Liz's parents yelled and screamed a lot at each other, especially when they had started drinking, they seldom became physically violent with each other. They seemed to prefer to treat their offspring to this instead.

During the parents' sober times, life wasn't much better. Liz's mother had a perfectionist streak and would swear and scream at her children if they dirtied any part of her house. The message they all heard loud and clear was that a clean house was more important than they were.

Before leaving home at age fifteen, Liz truly believed she would never be able to do anything right, and that she was a huge burden to everyone due to her medical weaknesses. She became convinced that she was totally unlovable and deserved nothing good.

For the next several years, Liz moved from one friend's home to the next. Most of the time her reason for moving was that her friend's father, brother, or uncle forced her to have sex with them. They would make her feel that this was the payment for her room and board.

By the time Liz left her teens behind, she had been consistently and repeatedly used, abused, and thrown away. She entered her twenties determined never to trust anyone ever again, especially men. She was already a mother herself and decided that come what may, her daughter Stephanie would never feel the rejection and self-loathing she herself had felt growing up.

The only person Liz had any warm feelings towards was her paternal grandmother. Liz loved to tell stories about her visits with this special woman who seemed to have shown her real love, and had treated her in such a way that even the memories of this grandmother brings tears to her eyes. Her relationship with her gran instilled a deep, lasting love for the elderly.

At the age of twenty, with a two-year-old child, Liz landed a job in a nursing home. This nursing home also had a daycare attached to it, so she was able to get a spot there for Stephanie. Two blocks from this home she discovered an aunt of hers, whom she hadn't seen since she was a tiny girl herself. Liz and her daughter soon fell into the routine of visiting with her aunt after work. Her aunt welcomed her and offered her a couple of rooms in her home until she could really get on her feet and decide what she wanted from life.

With her aunt's emotional and practical support, Liz thoroughly enjoyed working with the seniors during the daytime hours. During the evenings she completed her high school credits and applied to medical school, never expecting to be accepted.

When her acceptance letter arrived, Liz discovered she had a host of emotions that she couldn't ever remember feeling before. There was the natural excitement followed closely by doubt and self-doubt. She kept hearing childhood phrases in her head like, "You're a nobody;" or, "You'll never amount to anything;" or, "You're not smart enough and will only fail, so why even try?" or, "Your health will stop you from doing anything worthwhile anyway;" or, "Who do you think you are?"

Liz's aunt encouraged her to let all the emotions have a

voice and get them out into the open. Once her childhood messages had been verbalized and examined, she was able to get a glimpse of the lies they represented. Finding all of these emotions too overwhelming, Liz seemed to fight her way back to logic and tried to push the emotions back inside the "vault" to deal with sometime in the future.

A week before her thirty first birthday, Liz had not only graduated in the top ten percent of her class, but had also finished her internship and was ready to make a home for herself and Stephanie. As Liz recalls these years, she gets the same kind of misty eyes when talking about her aunt that she gets when talking about her grandmother. Liz's aunt not only supported and encouraged her, but also taught her how to begin to trust again, how to love and be loved, how to hope, and how to share all of that with her daughter.

A week after her graduation, Liz was invited to a party by friends of a friend of the person celebrating his thirtieth birthday. That's where she met Brad.

Now let me introduce you to Amy and James.

Amy is an adopted child. Her biological mother was only fourteen when she was born, and her parents insisted that Amy be given up for adoption. Amy has an older brother who is the biological son of her adoptive parents. Her brother is five years older than she is.

Being a highly intelligent girl, it didn't take Amy long to discover that to be female really sucked! She watched her mother cower every time her father came into the room. She heard her father constantly yell at her mother for being "a stupid cow," and blaming her for everything that went wrong in their house.

At family functions, the ever observant Amy would watch

her grandfathers (on both sides) treat her grandmothers the same way. Her uncles also treated their wives in the same unjust manner.

Amy quickly learned to despise females for what she perceived as their weaknesses, but struggled with the fact that she too was female.

By the time Amy was five or six, her older brother would often crawl into bed with her and touch her in private areas and make her touch him. The whole thing made her want to vomit, and she often scrubbed her skin with SOS pads to try and clean off the filth she felt. The ever thinking little girl wanted to run to her mother and tell her everything, but reasoned that her weak mother wouldn't be able to do anything anyway. With her limited understanding, she slotted what was happening in the "weak female" compartment of her mind.

Having been born with her biological grandmother's stubborn determination, Amy decided not to talk about what went on in her bedroom when the adults assumed she was asleep. She kept all of this abuse inside, where over the years it turned into silent rage. She felt she couldn't trust anyone. She believed she was alone in this world and would have to learn to look after herself.

Around the age of seven or eight, Amy's mother noticed the attention her son was giving his sister. This caused a great deal of jealousy, and from that moment on Amy couldn't do anything right. Her mother constantly criticized her for: not setting the table just right, for not washing the dishes correctly, for the clothes she wore, for the way she would sit or stand...well, the list could take up several pages!

This constant criticism, which is a form of abuse, was added to Amy's garbage dump inside. The garbage began to ferment, and it was harder and harder to maintain control of the fierce anger that was growing. This anger displayed itself in periods of deep sadness. This deep sadness would turn into bouts of depression. These bouts of depression turned into throwing herself colossal pity parties where overeating became her only comfort. This overeating turned into self-loathing that turned into more anger and more to dump onto the garbage heap.

At age thirteen, Amy had already developed her figure, as well as a reputation for being an easy lay.

Her brother's secret sex life with her continued until he told her she was nothing but a big, fat, lazy slob and her body disgusted him. Since Amy wasn't his real sister, he convinced himself that there was nothing wrong with what he had been doing.

For the next twenty years, Amy's life seemed to be a constant series of conflict. She decided to throw herself into her chosen career and focus on the climb up the proverbial ladder. After several years of hard work, Amy succeeded in becoming the CEO of a thriving finance consulting firm. She never allowed anyone to get emotionally close to her and developed the life philosophy, "Get on board or get out of my way."

During her career rise, Amy's personal life and choice in boyfriends seemed to go from weak to wimpy. In her determination never to be victimized ever again, Amy always clung to being the controller in all her personal, as well as professional, relationships. Amy always needed to know where her boyfriend was, who he was talking to, and what was being said. She was always suspicious of times he spent away from her, and would throw accusations around until he would pack up and leave. There were even a few times when Amy's boyfriend at the time would lose control and beat her up before leaving.

At the age of thirty-five, Amy began to get desperate for a

husband and a baby. Friends and colleagues had told her from time to time that her overbearing personality was a deterrent for meeting the kind of man she was looking for. As a result, Amy reverted to the weak female role she so despised, but figured she was more likely to attract someone less wimpy.

As the keynote speaker at a business luncheon, Amy was seated beside James, who had organized the event. There seemed to be an instant connection between the two, at least in the areas of finance and retirement goals.

James is his mother's oldest child. He is his father's middle child. James has a younger half-sister and half-brother on his mother's side, and an older half-brother and a younger stepbrother on his father's side.

James' mother's first marriage was to a divorced man who had a young son he hardly ever saw.

When James was close to three years old, he remembers hearing his parents screaming at each other a lot. As these screaming matches increased, his father's "at home time" decreased.

James remembers that often the only time he felt safe was when he was hiding under his bed! He even remembers keeping a supply of snacks hidden inside a stuffed dog's zippered belly. He comments that often he was under the bed so long he would get hungry. His parents' drinking and yelling often meant he got no supper, so his hidden stash became extremely important.

Not long after his third birthday, James' father just disappeared. His mother didn't talk to James about his father and his father never came to see him. James remembers wondering what he had done that was so bad to make his father leave without even saying good-bye. Secretly, James blamed his mother, but was afraid to say anything for fear that she would leave as well. This is probably the time James began to swallow his anger and learned to pretend that everything was just fine.

Soon after his father had left, James started to hear the same belittling comments levied at him that had always been hurled at his father. His mother seemed to expect James to start doing the "man-type" jobs around the house without being shown how. Then he would be screamed at for not doing it the right way.

Two years later, his mother remarried and within a year presented him with a baby brother, and two years after that he was introduced to his baby sister. In all that time there had been no word from his own father.

By his tenth birthday, James often found the parental responsibility for his siblings handed over to him. While his parents drank or smoked-up, he would open a can of pork and beans (or whatever he could find) and feed the three of them their supper. Then he would make sure they didn't provoke their parents into a violent attack by keeping his brother and sister hidden in his room until it was safe to put them to bed.

On his tenth birthday, James remembers the doorbell ringing. His mother went to answer it with himself close behind her. On the shabby porch stood a man holding a brand new shiny, red bike. Looking around his mother, the man spoke to James and wished him a happy birthday. Before James could respond, his mother's face turned an ugly purple color, and a long, loud barrage of foul names spat out at this stranger on the porch. James wondered what this man had done, but wouldn't trade places with him for anything.

From the little James was able to catch, it appeared that this stranger was James' "no-good" father. The message James remembers receiving during this public display of loathing was: His father was a no-good, stinking man, and that it had been a huge mistake for her to have married him; therefore, James too must be a huge, stinking mistake! No wonder his mother didn't seem to like him!

Peeking around his voluptuous mother, James tried to get a look at this man who apparently was his father, and according to his mother, the worst human being on the face of this planet.

After what seemed to be a very long screaming match, James' father plunked the bike down and tried to say good-bye to his son, but soon gave up and vanished yet again.

After this unforgettable display, James felt a deep sadness inside that grew each time he rode his new red bike or saw his friends with their fathers. This too had to be swallowed because he knew there would be major trouble if he ever even mentioned his father in his mother's presence.

By the time James was twelve, he had already started sneaking liquor from his parents' supply cabinet. It wasn't long before James started to steal cigarettes and other drugs that seemed to be so readily available around the house.

By his thirteenth birthday, James was no longer a virgin and well on his way to developing some serious addictions.

During his teens, James' addictions to drugs, alcohol, and cigarettes had fully taken hold, and he didn't care how or where he got what he needed to get high or drunk or laid.

Even through these turbulent years, James' sense of responsibility for his brother and sister never wavered. He knew what was the right thing to do and had no difficulty telling his siblings, but it became harder and harder for him to follow his own advice.

Shortly after his sixteenth birthday, James met Sue through a mutual friend of her brother's.

To James, Sue was his answer to easy and frequent sex!

James had stopped feeling a long time ago, so he wouldn't have been able to allow himself to get in touch with them over a female.

Three weeks into his relationship with Sue, she disclosed that she was pregnant.

When Sue presented the pregnancy problem to him in the midst of tears and seeming bewilderment, he remembers sensing the world caving in on him. Shortly after being told he was going to be a father, Sue's father started screaming at him to do the right—manly—thing. James remembers his mind returning to his very early years and hearing his mother scream for him to do the right—manly—thing. He remembers feeling the same sense of bewilderment and confusion as to what the right—manly—thing really was and who would be able to show him.

James felt the same sense of entrapment, filled with the sense of obligation to comply that had been present in him for the majority of his life.

Even with all of James' seeming worldly knowledge, he was extremely naïve in so many ways. He never even considered the possibility that Sue's baby might not be his. If he had, the next couple of decades of his life would have been very different.

James and Sue's city hall wedding ceremony more closely resembled a funeral service. For his honeymoon, James stayed stoned and drunk for the entire weekend getaway.

Throughout Sue's pregnancy, James remembers little else than the inside of his favorite bar and the feel of hot liquor sliding down his throat. When he did manage to make his way up to the apartment that was now supposed to be his home, all he remembers are Sue's constant accusations and demeaning comments that reminded him of what his mother always hurled at his father.

James talks about sitting in the hospital coffee shop, trying to sober up before heading up to maternity for the delivery of his child. He talks about having a heart-to-heart with himself over changes he would need to make now that he was about to become a father. Again, he wondered how and if anyone was going to show him. From past experience, James assumed that this too he would probably have to figure out for himself.

Holding the tiny baby girl he believed was his in his arms for the first time, James talks about feelings that were unfamiliar to his heart. For the first time in his life he knew he would do whatever it took to protect and love this beautiful child. He knew that this probably also meant that he would take whatever he needed to from his wife to be this infant's daddy. He couldn't imagine anything becoming serious enough to make him disappear like his father had.

James soon fell back into a familiar care giver role. This time instead of hiding his charge in his room, he took her with him as much as possible. As an insurance salesman, he rearranged his work schedule so he could walk her to and from school. He tried as much as possible to be home until his daughter was asleep to shield her from his wife's vicious attacks.

Feeling frustrated over James' lack of connection to her, Sue quickly realized that in order to get to James she would have to go through her own daughter. She started with subtle comments about how his daughter didn't seem to resemble him at all. When all of Sue's attempts to separate James from their child failed, she began her direct attacks on her own daughter. These attacks mostly occurred after James had left his sleeping daughter in her bed and gone out to his various evening appointments. For no apparent reason, upon his return, James would find his little girl unable to breathe or passed out. The mutual concern for their daughter seemed to set aside some of the unpleasantness between James and Sue for a short period of time. But not long after the crisis passed, things would return to their former "normal" state. Shortly after that, their daughter would have another, often worse, episode.

One evening James had to return home for some papers he had forgotten. Quietly peeking into his daughter's room to ensure himself that she was fine, he saw Sue with a pillow over their daughter's face.

The quick thinking business mind sprang into action by pulling his ever-ready camera from his pocket and snapped a picture of the loving mother in her act. This photo evidence helped to convict Sue and gave sole custody of their child to James.

Throughout the legal procedures Sue disclosed that James was not her daughter's biological father.

James talks about a primal anger deep inside of him that came close to escaping at this disclosure. He talks about conflicting emotions all vying for supremacy, some releasing him from the trap that Sue and her family had set for him, some denying the claim, placing it on her "must hurt James'" pile of garbage. Some he recognized as a profound sadness that the one and only person that he truly loved might be taken from him.

Slowly standing to his feet and taking a deep breath, James looked straight at the judge and said, "Your Honor, everything inside of me tells me that this little girl is most definitely my daughter."

With Sue no longer a threat, James and his daughter fell into a comfortable routine. Working out of his home helped keep childcare expenses down. A warm, grandmotherly woman, who lived across the hall from them, agreed to sit with his daughter whenever James needed to see clients in the evening.

For the next several years, life continued on in this peaceful way. James loved watching his daughter grow. He loved the new business challenges coming his way. He loved the people he met at the various business luncheons that he attended so much that he soon found himself on the committee to organize these luncheons with the business community in his city.

It was at one of these business luncheons that James found himself seated beside Amy, the keynote speaker for the day.

Chapter 5
Living with the Power and Control Personality

This chapter focuses primarily on the victim mentality and their incredible talent of walking on egg shells without ever breaking any. This is a tricky and learned behavior that is absolutely necessary for their survival and the survival of their children.

Reading through chapter two and looking at the tools the power and control personality regularly uses to maintain a feeling of supremacy is not an easy thing to do. However, it does seem to be the first step to reversing this learned behavior.

If you have been told you are a power and controller, keep reading. The better you understand yourself and what your partner sees, the better chance you have of reversing this negative behavior.

If you are primarily in the role of the victim, you too have been exposed to and taught a distorted set of rules that seem to have become your belief system. This too can be unlearned and turned into healthy behavior that neither degrades yourself or your partner.

Let's follow the power and control wheel around and take a

glimpse behind closed doors as we see how our couples dealt with power and control when they were predominantly alone.

The following examples of power and control at work are only a tiny sample of what really went on behind closed doors.

Isolation:
Brad and Liz:

A month after they were married, Brad accepted a position in a law firm in another province without consulting Liz, thus forcing both Liz and her daughter to uproot and leave their family and friends.

Amy and James:

Shortly after they were married, Amy convinced James to start their own financial consulting firm. As a result, they worked together, lived together, and at times played together. This left little time for James to spend with his daughter, who became a latch key kid and spent many hours alone in their new home.

Belittling:
Brad and Liz:

After Brad announced that they were moving to the other end of the country, Liz tried to present him with the whole picture regarding her job, her daughter's schooling, friends, and family that lived close by. When she had finished, Brad came back with, "I want you to stay home anyway and be my little homemaker. I've never wanted a working wife. Besides, I want a couple of kids of our own soon, so you won't have time to play at doctoring."

Amy and James:

Shopping for and setting up their new offices, James was continuously reminded that he didn't have any sense of color or style or vision or organizational ability. James soon began to swallow his own ideas about how he envisioned their new office space because he realized Amy would just dismiss them anyway.

Blame:

Brad and Liz:

Finding herself exhausted from packing up her home, traveling across the country, and starting the long, tedious task of unpacking, Liz reminded Brad that it had been his choice they all move, so some help from him would be appreciated. Brad stood to his feet, marched over to stand directly in front of her, and accused her of being a lazy, complaining bitch and she had better get used to doing everything on her own. When Liz started to protest, the blood vessels in Brad's eyes seemed to pop, and he grabbed her by the throat and started choking her. When he finally let go and Liz slumped to the floor, he loomed over her, wagging his finger in her face and screamed, "Look what you made me do!"

Amy and James:

Being in the stepmother position was hard for Amy. She was used to insisting that she always came first, no matter what. James' daughter resented Amy for taking almost all of her father's time and wasn't at all willing to accept this interloper into her life. In a desperate attempt to gain acceptance (or was it supremacy?), Amy tried to buy her way into her stepdaughter's heart. This only seemed to add resentment and increased the lack of respect towards her stepmother.

Trying to talk to James about her growing sense of being disrespected by his daughter, she started to accuse him of not wanting her to be close to his precious daughter, of being jealous of her, and blaming him for not making his daughter treat her, his wife, with respect.

Threats:
Brad and Liz:
Whenever Liz would speak her mind about an issue, Brad would either turn to alcohol or leave the house for days at a time. He would never let her know where he was or when he would be home, and substantial withdrawals would be made from their bank account. Brad would just arrive home after work one night as if nothing ever happened, but the money was never redeposited into their joint account or the issues discussed.

Liz would often try to steer the conversation towards home, and found it hard to keep her longing to return to her family and friends out of her voice. She even suggested that Stephanie and her go for a visit during summer vacation. Brad would always find reasons that would make it impossible for a visit home until maybe sometime later.

Less than a year after moving to this remote little town, a drunken Brad hissed at Liz, "If you even think of leaving me, I'll kill your daughter in front of you and then do you."

Amy and James:
If James tried to reason with Amy and get her to see his point of view, especially where his daughter was concerned, Amy seemed to get in touch with the little girl inside of her that could do nothing right. This seemed to tap into her massive insecurities and had the ability to produce such rage in her that

she would pick up any breakable object and hurl it at the wall right beside James. James would often slide down to sit on the floor, covering his head, waiting for the barrage to finish.

Fear:
Brad and Liz:
Approximately one half hour before Brad was due to walk through the door, Liz's stomach started to lurch. Her eyes skidded to all the areas in her house that Brad had ever beaten her for not having it to his liking, and found herself running around making sure that everything was the way he wanted them to be. She found herself setting and resetting the table for dinner several times, polishing the flatware and glasses, and even rewashing dishes, hoping everything would be to his liking.

Amy and James:
James always seemed to need to be the referee between his wife and his daughter, while trying hard not to be disloyal to either. As a result, he developed ulcers and began to dread going home. The moment he turned the corner onto his street, his ulcer would flare up and attack. He never knew what he would find on the other side of his own door.

Helplessness:
Brad and Liz:
The day after yet another black eye, along with many other bruises, Brad came home in the middle of the day with a huge bouquet of flowers and a sheepish look on his face. Giving Liz the flowers, he appeared close to tears as he reiterated his promise that he would get help and it would never happen again. Getting down on the floor in front of her, he asked if she could give him another chance.

For Liz, this side of Brad reminded her of the person she had fallen in love with. His seeming earnest plea yanked at her maternal instincts to help him.

Amy and James:

Amy seemed to sense when James was coming to the end of his considerable patience with her. That's when she would revert to her wounded little girl persona. A frustrating James would inevitably return to doing the right—manly—thing and dig even deeper inside for even more patience to deal with his overbearing, yet helpless, wife/child.

During these periods Amy would often seek counselling.

Guilt:
Brad and Liz:

After yet another beating, another woeful, apologetic Brad, another peace offering gift, another promise to get help, without any change happening, Liz would start packing her bags. Brad would loiter in the hall and finally come into their room with a deep sigh and plop on the bed trying to catch her eye. Brad, the charmer, would reappear and announce his undying love for her and finish with, "I guess you never really loved me if you could just walk away from me this easily."

Amy and James:

Whenever James and his daughter came to the end of their ability to cope with all the verbal and nonverbal attacks from Amy, they would close ranks and become even closer, making Amy feel even more like an outsider. This familiar feeling for Amy sent her into her inner child where she alternated between pouting and trying to please. This approach invariably brought feelings of guilt to both father and daughter who vowed to try even harder.

I Am Right:
Brad and Liz:

Whenever Brad had backed himself into a corner and was forced to follow through with counselling, he would spin his story in such a way that the counsellor asked to see Liz and her daughter for some sessions as well. Using this approach, Brad could actually make himself believe that he really wasn't to blame for the state of their marriage. He could easily shift the responsibility on to Liz and her history of allowing herself to be victimized, thus allowing the "I am right" mentality to reign.

Amy and James:

In their business world, Amy often failed to share vital information with James. As a result, when he spoke to a customer or to other employees, she would be able to jump in to correct him, making him look like an idiot and herself the source of all knowledge.

The need to be "right" was so strong in Amy that she would go to great lengths to prove every detail, even when those she needed to prove her "rightness" to had ceased to care a longtime back in the conversation.

Children:
Brad and Liz:

Brad's abstruse lawyer mind loved to use the divide and conquer method between Liz and her daughter. He would lavish her daughter with gifts and attention and would encourage her to talk about her preteen issues with her mom, and together they would snicker about her mother's values or behavior. As a result, mistrust was developed between mother and daughter.

Amy and James:

Amy started to treat James' daughter much like her own mother had treated her, i.e. always redoing her chores, always pointing out the negatives in everything his daughter did or wore.

If James tried to address any of these issues with her, she would attack his seeming inability to parent correctly with a great deal of exasperation in her voice.

Finances:

Brad and Liz:

Brad explained to Liz that as his law practice was growing, he didn't have the time to handle their personal finances as well, so she would have to take this over for him. At first Liz was flattered that Brad thought her capable, even though math had never been one of Liz's strengths.

As Liz paid bills and maintained their home, she soon discovered that what she believed should have been in their joint account was often way short of what was really there. When she questioned Brad about the difference, he informed her that since he worked, it was his money and he could withdraw whatever he wanted. When she tried to reason with him that that made it impossible for her to keep an accurate account, he only got angry and started calling her a stupid cow and to stop blaming him for her inadequacies.

Liz soon discovered that her keeping the books only gave Brad more fuel to blame and belittle her, not to mention threaten and instill fear.

Amy and James:

Amy determined that she was much better at bookkeeping than James, so she kept a very tight rein on both the business and household finances. James' daughter had to earn her allowance to Amy's satisfaction. Amy insisted that she was trying to instill a sense of gratitude in James's daughter, as she felt that he had rather spoiled her.

Amy had to approve any of James' expenses. Resentment brewed under the surface for both father and daughter, as they felt powerless to change the way things were. Once again, James felt the familiar sense of feeling trapped!

Rules Always Change:
Brad and Liz:
Liz kept trying to get back into the practice of medicine. Whenever she spoke to Brad about taking a position at the local hospital's ER, he would verbally encourage her. Yet the very next day he would add several chores to her list of responsibilities, making it virtually impossible for her to get to the hospital to see about her return to her profession. Whenever Liz explained to Brad that he gave her too many running around errands to do, he would come back with a remark like, "At least no one's life is in danger due to your incompetence."

Amy and James:
Trying hard to win James' daughter's affection, Amy often encouraged her to borrow her jewelry or articles of clothing.

One day Amy was away on a short business trip, and James' daughter borrowed her diamond earrings for a night out with her boyfriend. When Amy returned unexpectedly, she caught James' daughter heading out the door wearing her earrings. It would be hard to believe that the whole neighborhood didn't hear what an ungrateful, sneaky, disrespectful daughter James had by the tongue lashing Amy gave him.

As a result, James' daughter's evening was totally ruined,

and she never ever again borrowed anything from her wicked stepmother.

Stalking:
Brad and Liz:

Liz began to get paranoid regarding the sense that she was being followed all the time. It seemed no matter where she went, Brad knew all about it.

One day Liz was late getting home from a doctor's appointment. As she fumbled for her house keys, she heard the phone ringing inside. By the time she got in and ran to answer it, somehow knowing it was Brad, all she heard was a dial tone. Her stomach started to lurch, as she knew to expect trouble when Brad came home. Sure enough, as soon as he barged through the door he started hurling accusations at her such as, "Where were you?" "Who were you with?" "You're nothing but a __ slut."

Amy and James:

Getting their business off the ground meant a lot of hard work and some individual travel for both James and Amy.

At times James would have driven to a city an hour or so away and discover an important document missing from his briefcase. Baffled, as he was sure he had checked that everything he would need was in his briefcase, he would take a deep breath and knew he would have to call Amy to fax him a copy.

This sort of thing kept happening, meaning he had to continuously call Amy to have her bail him out. Or Amy kept calling him to let him know that she had found a document that he needed, and that she needed his room number in order to be able to fax him a copy. It wasn't long before James realized that this was Amy's way of keeping tabs on him.

Suspicious:

Brad and Liz:

One of the first things Brad would do as soon as he got home from the office was to scroll through the telephone to see who had called during the day and drill Liz about each call. If he wasn't satisfied with her answers, he would call the number and say something like, "You called here today, what did you want?"

Many times Liz would look for something in her purse only to find that Brad had taken it out for some reason. Brad regularly searched through Liz's purse to check every receipt and read any notes, as well as scan her daytimer entries. Liz soon discovered that nothing was truly hers. Nothing was safe from Brad's paranoia.

Amy and James:

Amy had a hard time allowing James to be alone with his own daughter, as she was convinced they were plotting against her all the time. Even though she verbally encouraged them to spend time together, she would go into a depressive slump if they actually made plans.

When they were out for an evening together, Amy would call James' cell phone frequently with the lamest questions. James knew that to simply turn his cell phone off would bring Amy down on them in person and only intensify her fear that the two of them were plotting some sort of destruction to Amy's life.

No Rights, No Voice:

Brad and Liz:

Brad systematically whittled away at Liz's self-worth in so many ways that this resulted in Liz constantly second-guessing any decision she made, no matter how trivial. Even though, logically, Liz knew she was an intelligent woman, she would be extremely careful how she said virtually anything. She consciously picked her words, the best time, and even the location to say what she needed to say. The reason for all of this caution was that she simply never knew whether Brad would hear her or make fun of her or let her know how profoundly stupid she was for raising this issue—whatever the issue—or would simply ignore her.

As a result, Liz truly began to believe that she had no right to voice an opinion, and even if she tried it wouldn't count anyway.

Amy and James:
Amy's public speaking ability developed an incredible skill in her to voice her own point of view on virtually every subject. Her need to always be right or appear to come out on top developed her ability to twist words or meanings so that the person she was addressing became very confused and usually ended up agreeing with Amy because it sort of, kinda, sounded right.

Amy used this same bewitching ability to twist words or meanings to her own liking in the home, causing both James and his daughter to feel powerless.

James soon realized that he only got in touch with his own thoughts and ideas when he was away on a business trip, away from Amy. He began to journal these thoughts so he wouldn't lose them once he got home and Amy put her slant on them, causing total confusion.

When his daughter left for college, James found himself scheduling more and more business trips. At home he just knew he had no rights and no voice, so he seldom dared to express his opinions.

Possession:

Brad and Liz:

Whenever Brad took Liz to a business function, he would make sure she had a new dress, new shoes, and got her hair done for the event—all to his liking. While he was mingling and introducing Liz to his colleagues, he would always add that she was a doctor, and would hurry on to a new topic if he thought she might be ready to disclose that she hadn't practiced since being married to Brad.

Liz said she felt like Brad's trophy that he would dust off and dress up just to show off to his friends and colleagues.

Amy and James:

As their business grew, Amy would get more and more invitations to speak at business luncheons or conferences. Whenever possible, Amy wanted James to be present. Having a tall, dark, and maturely handsome male on her arm had a way of increasing her own self-worth. As a result, she was able to address the crowd with more confidence than when James wasn't present.

For James' part, he dreaded being "dressed for show" as he put it, but for the sake of peace, allowed himself to be paraded around to help build her confidence.

Manipulation:

Brad and Liz:

When Liz had finally come to the end of her tether, and had started to make plans to leave Brad and return to her home province, Brad called CAS (Children's Aid Society) and accused her of mistreating her daughter.

With CAS involvement, it took Liz several months to get out from under all the red tape and continue her plan of escape. This time however, she kept her plans well hidden from Brad.

Amy and James:

Whenever Amy sensed that James was coming to the end of his patience with her behavior and disrespect for him, she would plan a great celebration to honor a milestone in James' life. These parties so confused him, yet reminded him of the Amy he had fallen in love with, oh so long ago.

James again got in touch with his fierce need to do the right—manly—thing, causing him to dig even deeper for more patience and understanding to deal with his insecure wife/child.

Chapter 6
Reversal for the Power and Control Personality

The power and control personality is predominantly something that is learned within the home environment! The great thing about anything that is learned is that it can be unlearned. It comes down to choice!

The power and control personality generally harbors an enormous amount of anger. When asked to describe their anger, the power and control personality usually has a hard time putting words to the feelings. They just know they are extremely angry most of the time. Often they are only able to identify that at the root of their anger is a tremendous sense of injustice that they need to guard against.

This anger is seldom analyzed, but often acted out. The power and control personality often expresses their anger by choosing some of the following:

• Choosing a form of substance abuse, i.e. drugs, alcohol, sex, tobacco, etc.

• Choosing to lash out at the society they feel left out of, often causing them to get in trouble with the law.

• Choosing to have difficulty with anyone in authority,

causing him or her not to focus or follow their employer's instructions, which causes a lot of job-hopping.

• Choosing to find a victim mentality as a partner, causing the cycle to continue.

Once the power and control personality gets to the place where they can actually admit that they are angry and need help, they can finally move on to doing something constructive about their anger.

The following exercise helps pull anger apart so it can be understood, and change can start to take place.

Anger Model* I

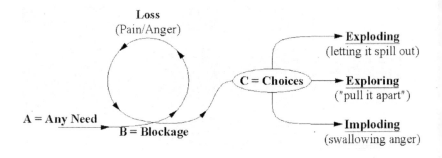

*Redeveloped from B. D. Boeckner's book, *AngerWorks*, page 58.

As you follow Amy through the anger model, watch her thought process.

Amy and James:

Amy, who didn't have children of her own, always found herself angry and hurt when she was unable to control James' daughter. The harder she tried, the more explosive she became when James' daughter didn't cooperate. The more she exploded, the more threatening she became. The more threatening she became, the more James' daughter pulled away from her. The more she pulled away, the angrier Amy became.

That's what finally brought Amy and James to seek counselling, and where we started to unravel Amy's anger. The above exercise was one of the tools we used to "pull apart" Amy's anger so she could begin to understand it. Once the deeper core issue (like anger) is exposed and understood, then Amy could decide what she was going to do with her new knowledge. It became her choice to change or not to change!

The following is working through the above exercise. Hopefully, as you continue to read you will get a clearer idea of how this exercise works.

Amy's Need:
I need James' daughter to need me like a mother.

Losses/Fears (need not being met):
1. Can't be a parent
2. Can't give advice
3. Control
4. Acceptance
5. Love
6. Losing
7. Respect—from his daughter
8. Self-respect

9. Significance
10. Security

The next step is to put feelings to the list of losses/fears that cause the anger. Envision this page and the last side-by-side, and follow each issue from need to losses/fears to feelings, then right through to reality.

Feelings:

1. Empty
2. Unheard
3. Helpless
4. Sad and lonely
5. Sad and lonely
6. Frustrated
7. Hurt
8. Low self-esteem
9. Worthless
10. Feel like a lost child

My Reality:

1. I'm not her parent.
2. It's not my place.
3. I've never really had control.
4. She hasn't rejected all of me.
5. I can't lose what I never really had.
6. It's not a contest.
7. Respect has to be earned.
8. I've alway struggled with this.
9. My self-worth is not dependent on the actions or opinions of anyone else.
10. I will never believe others love me until I have learned to love myself.

To help you understand what Amy has done in this exercise, let's have a closer look at the Anger Model I (found at the beginning of this chapter).

This ABC of understanding your anger model takes you from the moment you recognize you are angry right through to the choice you make in dealing with your anger.

Often there is only a fraction of a second between the moment you recognize your anger and your response to it. The anger model *forces* you to look more closely at your anger. If you look at Amy's anger background, her usual pattern of choice seemed to be to explode whenever anger was present.

Exploding is a choice many power and control personalities seem to like to use. The person, who chooses to explode when angry, often appears to be walking around looking for the next thing to be angry at.

The exploder often suffers from high blood pressure, anxiety attacks, and would be more susceptible to heart attacks or strokes. These negatives may seem to be worthwhile, if by exploding their needs are being met.

The next time you explode, take an inventory of what your entire body is doing. How your legs, arms, neck, jaw, etc. all get involved.

Most of the time when the exploder is "letting it all out," those who are the recipients of their explosion have learned to tune them out. The sense that "here they go again" prevails as they roll their eyes heavenward in silence. Thus the exploder isn't really heard nor are their needs being met.

Imploding is a choice often made by those with a victim mentality. They have learned that anger is unacceptable and will most likely get them into trouble; therefore, they have learned how to swallow it or push it deep down inside. The main difficulty with this approach is what happens when there is no room left? Often when the imploder gets to the "full" stage, it will be something extremely minor that finally makes them blow. At that point everything inside will come tumbling out. When the imploder finally explodes, they invariably act out of character. As a result, those around only see the trivial issue that seemingly caused the explosion, shake their heads and tell the imploder to get a grip. This often causes the imploder to sink into a deeper depression.

Healthwise, the imploder is often in danger of developing ulcers, high blood pressure, and lives in a constant state of anxiety. This anxiety often turns to depression because the anger that remains buried inside festers and causes deep, deep sadness.

Choosing this method of dealing with anger does not get the imploder's needs met.

Exploring is a much healthier choice in dealing with your anger. It opens up a window of time where you can start asking yourself some very important questions. I call it my "five-minute window." The moment you find yourself angry, you put the five-minute window in place.

The five-minute window forces you to mentally stop before reacting. Once stopped, you start asking questions like: 1) What is really ticking me off? 2) What need(s) in me are not being met? 3) What is familiar about this situation? 4) What is familiar about the way this makes me feel?

As you learn to ask yourself the tough questions, your list will grow and grow.

As you master this exercise, the five-minute window (or whatever time suits you) will become second nature to you. The byproduct of this exercise is getting to know yourself from the inside out, as well as getting to understand what your anger truly is all about. You will find that the issue that is causing the anger is invariably hooked to something in the past.

Using the exploring method takes you right back to *A = Any Need Not Being Met.*

At the "any need" part of this exercise you will learn how to "pull apart" and discover what need(s) you really have that are not being met. This means you have to go deeper than the obvious or surface reasons. You do this by asking the tough questions during the five-minute window.

Notice what Amy eventually put down as her need. In order to get to this core need, she had to peel back the various layers. For instance, some of the layers she had to acknowledge were: 1) I need James' daughter to accept me as his wife. 2) I'm the adult, she's the child, and I need her to obey me. 3) I need her to know and except how much I have to offer.

While this tearing apart was going on, Amy was constantly confronted with her true feelings. As a result, she finally broke down and shouted, "I just want her to need me to be her mother." Voila, we finally got the core need.

Amy was using her need to be needed and turning it into a power and control struggle that affected not only herself, but James and his daughter as well.

First, Amy had to come to that difficult place where she had to acknowledge that whatever approach she had been using wasn't working. Then, she had to come to the place of realizing she needed to change. Lastly, she would have to ask for some help.

Peeling down to her core need brought Amy face to face with her own insecurities. The very thing she had been trying to hide and/or run away from. Hidden behind the bullying was the controlling insistence that she actually did know everything about everything.

Blocks are what stops your needs from being met.

As soon as you have peeled down to your core need, you begin to realize that fear is present. Fear of what? Included in that fear is a fear of the past. In other words, your present unmet need reminds you of your history, which brings back painful memories. Another fear that hits you right between the eyes is your fear or sense of losing something. This sense of loss is actually the anger producer.

In Amy's case, she was reminded that she had not been able to have children of her own. She was also reminded of her own mother's harsh words and being told to get out of her sight over and over during her childhood. Along with these memories, Amy felt the pain of rejection, as well as the reminder that she could do nothing right.

Watch what losses (or fear of losses) Amy gets in touch with. Each of her ten losses brings its own pain and hurt, which is at the root of the anger felt.

As Amy makes herself accountable for her own sense of loss and the fear connected to that loss, she can then allow herself to feel the pain involved.

This is not an easy exercise, but a very worthwhile one as it helps you face your *real* issues.

Lastly, we went through a reality check.

When anger is present, the whole world seems to be out of focus. It's rather like, in your anger, you are looking at the situation wearing my very strong eyeglasses. I guarantee you that the situation will look very blurry and out of focus. Taking a reality check is in essence like taking a step back, putting your own glasses back on, and looking at the situation as it really is.

As you follow each one of Amy's losses through to her feelings about that loss, right on to her reality check, you find her beginning to make sense of her emotions.

Instead of her anger controlling her, she is beginning to get a handle on what her anger is really all about. In making herself go through this step, she is in fact turning the tables and beginning to control her own anger.

To Be a Man:

Looking at the two outer rings of the following wheel, we are reminded of the power and control wheel in chapter two.

The two outer rings often represent what a power and control personality feels and/or believes about himself.

The two inner rings give us a hint at how the outer ring characteristics need to be completely turned around. The power and control personality's view of life and himself needs a complete overhaul.

For a man who has clung to the beliefs that are represented in the outer two rings to be able to get to a place where he allows himself to move towards what is represented by the inner two rings is quite a personal struggle. He, first of all, has to admit to the possibility that his view of strength, pride, supremacy, being his own person, the provider, in control, and pointing blame away from himself may be a distorted view. Once he has started to reevaluate these characteristics, he can gradually learn to: admit his weaknesses, learn to deal with shame, see himself through the eyes of others, take ownership for his own actions, become equal to his partner, be able to admit when he is wrong, learn to listen—really listen—to others, and be able to ask for help.

This transaction is risky, especially for the power and control personality. It is in essence building trust that has really never existed. Trust in your own ability to discover what you truly feel and believe, as well as trust that your partner will be able to support you in this journey. It is also a process and sometimes progress seems to be very slow. However, as trust is built, brick by brick, the risks are rewarded with a new awareness of who you really are and what being in a relationship actually means.

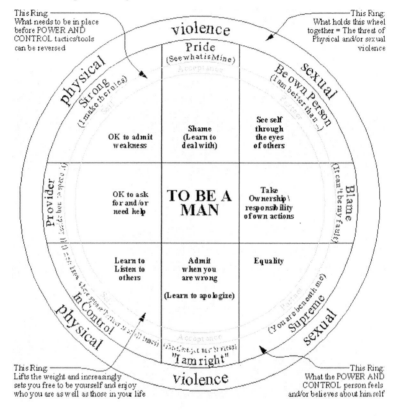

Men, as you begin to change, you will need to be very patient with your partner. Your partner is used to you readjusting and adding new tools to be used to keep her in line and guessing, so she might not immediately believe that you really want to change.

This is when couple counselling can be invaluable.

To Be a Woman:

The following wheel is very similar to the wheel on the previous page. There are some distinct differences however, so I wanted to be sure to address these differences.

The female power and control personality seems to love to use the old traditional female role as "housekeeper" as a weapon and/or excuse to dominate, bully, and control everyone who lives in her home.

The female power and control personality also seems to use her very gender as a powerful tool. Her own sexuality is very often used as a lure or reward for getting her partner to do exactly what she wants, when she wants, and how she wants.

The female power and control personality also needs to be willing to reevaluate her own beliefs and feelings about the characteristics mentioned in the outer two rings. As she allows herself to discover how her beliefs and feelings are distorted, she will gradually be willing to open herself up towards change.

Trust is also a major factor for the female power and control personality. As she is able to discover what she really believes and who she really is, she will be able to learn to trust her partner, as well as other people in her life.

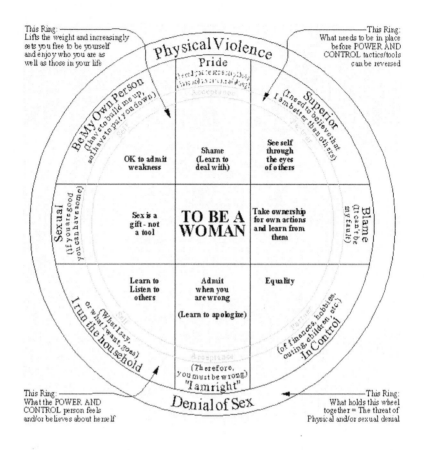

Women who truly want to change may have a hard time convincing their partners or solicit their support. Your partners have become used to the sudden changes, and have become extremely skeptical of these changes as they usually have been another way to isolate, to belittle, to blame, to threaten, etc. So be patient and communicate with your partner what you are learning about yourself.

Couple counselling is often a great step during this time of self-assessment.

Chapter 7
Reversing the Victim Mentality

Victim Reversal Strategies

Once the victim of power and control has started to fight back, either within the relationship or removed from the relationship, he/she often struggles with tremendous anger. This anger helps him/her get in touch with the injustice of the way he/she has been treated and can bring with it a new determination to never let anyone treat him/her like that ever again. This anger can be healthy, if it is used in a positive way, such as educating themselves in the area of both the power and control personality and the victim mentality. However, this anger can also create a new prison, as often the victim hangs on to their anger and refuses to forgive the power and control person in their lives. The main reason given is that they (the power and control personality) don't deserve to be forgiven, followed closely by they haven't asked for forgiveness.

The type of anger that is directly connected to the unwillingness to forgive does much damage and keeps the victim from truly being free to move on. Hanging on to this anger will continue to give control of your life to the very person you are most angry with. It may also subtly turn you into a power and control personality.

To Forgive or Not to Forgive, That is the Question!

The following illustration gives a glimpse of some lingering emotions that fester inside the victim if he/she chooses not to forgive.

You might ask, "How is it possible for me to forgive someone that has systematically tried to destroy every aspect of who I am?" I'm not indicating that forgiveness will be easy; however, forgiveness is a must if you, as the former victim, are truly going to set yourself free.

Forgiveness is a choice! Forgiveness is not so much a benefit for the power and control personality in your life as it is for yourself. To choose to forgive opens a channel for the anger inside to escape. It also opens a passage for all the positive emotions and sense of freedom to enter the very core part so you can begin to discover who you really are.

My own faith in God has helped me understand the importance of forgiveness. In the Bible, God says, "For if you forgive men when they sin against you, your heavenly Father will also forgive you." Matthew 6:14 (NIV).

Forgiveness often seems to be confused with feelings. "If I feel like it I will forgive," or "When I feel ready I'll forgive." Forgiveness is not a feeling, but an act of the will. It's a choice!

For me choosing to forgive started by actually saying the words out loud. Every time I got in touch with more anger, I again spoke the words of forgiveness out loud, choosing to open the channel for the anger to be able to escape my inner being. It wasn't long before I began to feel more joy and contentment. This change at the very core of who I really am seemed to be directly connected to being obedient and choosing to forgive the person(s) who had hurt me so very deeply.

The wonder of all of this is that the person(s) who injured me wasn't even present during my exercise in forgiving them.

Forgiveness brings freedom to yourself!

Unforgiveness leaves you locked up in a prison of your own making, to which you yourself hold the key.

Unforgiveness				Forgiveness	
R	Bitterness	**I**	**A**	Peace	
E	Upset - physically	**N**	**C**	Love	**L**
J	Stressed out	**J**	**C**	Contentment with self	
E	No peace	**U**	**E**	Joy	**I**
C	No joy	**S**	**P**	Comfort	
T	Anger	**T**	**T**		**F**
I	Fear	**I**	**A**	Positive feelings	
O	Wanting a 'drink'	**C**	**N**	Release	**E**
N	Trapped	**E**	**C**	Letting go	
			E		
PRISON				**FREEDOM**	

Working with the clients in the counselling room, I would write the words "Unforgiveness" and "Forgiveness" at the top of the blackboard. Then I would ask the client to get in touch with their feelings regarding not being willing or able to forgive. As I wrote their feelings down under unforgiveness (much like the exercise above), the weight of these feelings seemed to literally push them down deeper into the armchair. When the list of feelings seemed to be complete, I asked what held them in place. That's when the client would invariably get in touch with their intense fear of rejection and their fierce sense of injustice. It was as if these became the walls to hold all the angry feelings in place. The whole seemed to be a man-made, emotional prison that held them captive.

Once the client had gotten in touch with their sense of feeling boxed in, I would ask them what it might feel like if they would be able to forgive. As these feelings poured out, I wrote them down under forgiveness. As they allowed themselves to feel what forgiveness might be like, their whole countenance began to change. They would sit up straighter, they would be able to make eye contact, the deep stress lines seem to lift from their faces, and a glint of hope seemed to reach their eyes as I watched them try on the mantel of forgiveness.

Once their list seemed complete, I again asked what would hold these together for them. That's often when a deep inner sigh would escape and they would announce that then they would feel accepted and finally be able to live.

That's when freedom can rein.

Anger Exercise

Another strategy in dealing with pent-up anger is to "pull it apart."

Let's reconnect with one of our couples and walk through an anger exercise Liz did to help her understand the underlying causes of her anger.

Anger Model* II

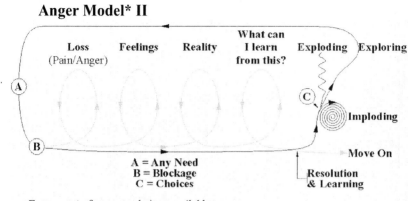

A = Any Need
B = Blockage
C = Choices

From onset of anger to choices available
From onset of anger to exploring choice back to point of anger

*Redeveloped from B. D. Boeckner's book, *AngerWorks*, page 58.

Brad and Liz:

Liz talked a lot about not feeling valued as a person by Brad. The only time she felt any sense of value was when she was on display at Brad's work parties or family gatherings. She stated how angry this would make her feel, adding how painful it was to be virtually invisible, especially to the man who claimed to love her.

This brought us to the above exercise.

Liz's Need:
I need not to be invisible to Brad.

Losses:

1. Self-respect
2. Respect for Brad
3. Self-worth
4. Dignity
5. Significant
6. Trust
7. Self
8. My freedom

Feelings:

1. Small
2. Angry
3. Insufficient
4. Out of focus
5. Trivial
6. Confused
7. Lost
8. Trapped

My Reality:

1. I haven't changed.
2. I don't respect him when he doesnt' see me.
3. I am a worthwhile person!
4. It's hard to know who I am.
5. Deep down I feel that I must be significant!
6. It's getting harder to trust Brad.
7. I used to know who I was and where I was going.
8. I am not in a prison cell. I hold the key to my own freedom.

What Can I Learn?

1. Brad is not the man I thought he was.
2. Respect needs to be earned; it cannot be demanded.

3. My self-worth is not dependent on how anyone chooses to treat me.

4. I can give myself permission to refocus on who I really am.

5. My significance comes from deep inside myself, not from anyone or anything outside of me.

6. Brad tells me to trust him, but his actions prove he isn't trustworthy.

7. I have given Brad the power to make me lose myself. I need to find a way to take back that power.

8. I can choose to forgive Brad and unlock my emotional prison door.

The above is a similar exercise to the one in Chapter six. Again, try following Liz's process from when she was able to recognize her core need right through to her sense of loss at her need not being met and how this made her feel. Then, watch as she gives herself a reality check and discovers what she can learn using this technique.

This is an exercise you can do for yourself. Next time you find yourself angry about something, try following Amy's (chapter six) and Liz's course through this valuable anger exercise.

Chapter 8
Relationship Equality

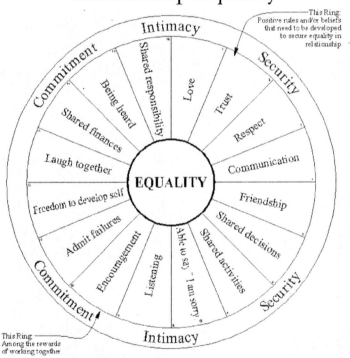

This Ring:
Positive rules and/or beliefs
that need to be developed
to secure equality in
relationship

This Ring:
Among the rewards
of working together

The Equality Wheel was redeveloped from the wheel put out by "Domestic Abuse Intervention Project" of Duluth, Minnesota.

As both the power and control wheel and the victim mentality wheel have been used to show the tools used and the beliefs or rules being adhered to, I wanted to continue with this theme and show what a positive, equal relationship might look like.

Notice that I've entitled the large inner ring "Positive Rules and/or Beliefs That Need to be Developed to Secure Equality in Relationships." This was done deliberately, as every relationship takes work and time to truly develop equality.

If you recognized yourself (or your partner) in the previous chapters, this wheel seems like something out of a fantasy world and just as unattainable.

If you recognized yourself (or your partner) in chapter two, where we looked at the power and control personality, the equality wheel will probably scare you. However, if you look at the outer ring of the equality wheel, it shows three of the rewarding characteristics that you have been striving for most of your adult life. Somehow these rewards keep escaping your grasp. Is it possible for you to admit that your methods of obtaining these characteristics aren't working? If your method isn't working, are you willing to try something new? When you are able to answer yes to both questions, you will find the inner strength needed for you to honestly look at yourself so that you can finally begin to achieve what you have been fighting for all your life.

The greatest challenge toward equality in relationships for those who are power and control personalities or have been the victims of power and control is recognizing that both parties need help. Neither of the above methods brings a sense of self or equality into your relationship.

In an ideal world your partner will be ready for change at the same time you are. However, you and I both know that the real world seldom works that way. So what do you do if you recognize change is needed but your partner doesn't?

If you have identified yourself as the victim mentality, then we have discussed the above question to some degree in chapter three.

If you have identified yourself as the power and controller, or keep hearing that you are from your partner, friends, or coworkers, you will need to begin by honestly answering yes to the questions asked earlier in this chapter. Once you have been able to answer these questions, you will probably need to find a good counsellor who will be able to help you unravel your own personal insecurities.

For the power and control personality, you will have to remember that your partner will remain skeptical for some time. He/she has learned to question what you say, your motives, and your hidden agenda for a very long time. Be patient, educate yourself, and work on your own inner issues.

Oh, and did I mention to be patient!?

Let's briefly look at the wedges on the Equality Wheel. You might be thinking, "What's to look at? They are self-explanatory." If that is so, what gets in the way of fulfilling them and truly developing and maintaining equality in your relationship?

Love:

Before either party in the relationship can begin to develop love, they each need to understand what they individually mean by love. Both participants in the relationship brought their own belief system regarding what love is for them into this partnership. In the counselling room I often get couples to do a genogram, which is a study of the family of origin (described further in chapter nine). The better you understand where you came from and what made you you, the better the choices you will be able to make to determine your future.

Love is **not** sex. It is **not**, "I can't do better than him/her." It is **not** providing a parent for your children. It is **not** two can live cheaper than one. It is **not** he/she is better than being alone. It is **not** needing someone to control. It is **not** walking on eggshells for fear of doing or saying the wrong thing.

Love **is** making love. It **is**, "My life is better with him/her in it." It **is** wanting to produce and/or provide for children in a healthy way. It **is** supporting each other and encouraging each other to become the best possible individual. It **is** trusting each other to always be there for you. It **is** planning and dreaming together and growing comfortable old together.

Trust:

Trust sounds so simple, yet is so hard for many people. Whether trust is easy or difficult depends a great deal on your own history where trust is concerned.

It also depends on your trust belief regarding people of the opposite sex. For example, if you grew up believing that women/men can't be faithful (usually sexually or emotionally), when you marry you will most likely expect your partner to become dissatisfied with you and start looking elsewhere. You might even become somewhat paranoid. Again, doing a genogram and tracing the trust issue would be helpful.

The New Webster's Concise Dictionary defines trust as: "a reliance on the integrity, veracity, or reliability of a person or thing."

Respect:

Most of us determine what respect is by observing our parents and how they treated each other during our growing up years. Tracing your sense of respect using the genogram method might answer some of your questions regarding your present relationship.

The New Webster's Concise Dictionary definition of respect is: "A high regard for and appreciation of worth; esteem."

Respect is a mutual attribute. It is earned and cannot be forced or demanded.

Communication:

To be communicative is to be ready and willing to talk and give information. This sounds so simple, doesn't it? Then why do so many couples come into my office saying, "He/she never talks?" Or I might hear, "Getting him/her to talk is like pulling teeth," or "He/she is so open and friendly with everyone else, but hardly ever says anything to me."

From years of observation, I believe that the greatest difficulty in communicating as couples is that often the message sent is not the message received. By this I mean that when your partner says something or asks something of you, you often hear criticism because that is what you expect. As a result, you only half listen and are already formulating your response. The result of this type of communication is utter confusion, which leads to a shutting down on both sides.

One of the phrases I ask couples to become familiar asking each other is, "Help me understand." Using this method opens the door for further communication with the invitation to help your partner understand what you are really saying or meaning. The flip side to using this technique for better communication is that if you ask your partner to help you understand what they really mean, then you really have to listen. No, really listen with more than just your ears. Listen also with your heart.

Friendship:

If your partner wasn't already your best friend when you married, he/she should be becoming your best friend as your relationship grows. The very word, friendship, indicates a mutual affection independent of sexual love or family love.

When something happens throughout your day, ask yourself whom you most want to share your story with. That's the person who is your best friend.

Shared Decisions:

If love, trust, respect, communication, and friendship are being developed in your relationship, the by-product often is being able to share. It is virtually impossible that one partner could arbitrarily make decisions that will affect the entire household if the above attributes are being developed.

In sharing, the weight is being redistributed and could involve: decision-making, planning activities, dealing with finances, or sharing household responsibilities (as seen on the Equality Wheel). If one person in the relationship carried all the weight of any of these, they would not only get extremely tired, but eventually it could crush them. An equal partnership means sharing everything!

Able to Say "I Am Sorry"

Part of loving is being able to admit wrongs without fear of condemnation!

Part of trusting is being able to trust your partner to accept an apology without the fear that your wrong is going to be added to the arsenal pile to be used against you later.

Part of respecting is being able to respect your partner enough to be honest without the fear of being made to feel less than a person. This also involves respect for self.

Part of communication is being able to open up about the good and bad without the fear of being judged. This comes easier to some types of personalities, but is vital for the healthy development of any relationship

Part of sharing is being able to honestly share your emotions regarding any situation, including when you have blown it without fear of retribution.

Listening:

Listening is a skill that seems hard to learn. We live in a society where listening could easily be added to the endangered personal skills list. The fact is, most people only partially listen, especially when their partner in doing the talking. One part of the brain seems to be sorting through the recent events database that has been stored, trying to determine which one is getting them into trouble. Another part is quickly sifting through what is being heard (not necessarily what is being said) to determine what needs fixing now. Yet another part is busy formulating a response to what you believe is being said.

With all those parts extremely active, how can true listening occur? To truly listen, eye contact needs to be made (with your partner not the TV), as well as learning to put all the above parts of your brain on the back burner—giving full attention to your partner and what they want you to hear.

True listening is dovetailed with love, trust, and respect. It involves knowing your partner so well that their body language says at least as much as their words.

If you aren't sure you really understand what their message is, don't be afraid to ask for clarification. Don't assume you know!

Encouragement:

On the power and control wheel a lot of the tools used bring discouragement to the victim mentality and the entire household. Part of the process needed to develop equality in your relationship is to reverse the negative tools and replace them with positive ones.

Encouragement is an extremely powerful tool that begins to tear down the negative structures that have been built up over the years.

Remember that this is a process; reversing the damage years of negativity has created takes time and deliberate hard work. Therefore, be patient and consistent, and little by little the positives will start to take hold and be believed.

Encouragement is not a one-time quick fix. It has to become a part of everyday life. It is meant to build up while also tearing down the old walls or beliefs.

Admit Failures:

One of the surest ways to be heard by your partner is to be able to admit failures. This is especially true for the (previously) power and controls personality, as this has always been extremely difficult for them to do. For the (previously) victim mentality, on the other hand, admitting failures has always been expected, even when what was admitted to wasn't their failure, but uttered out of fear or to keep peace.

This means that during the reversal process the power and control personality will need to learn to be very sensitive and not allow the (previously) victim mentality to admit to perceived failures that really aren't theirs. Don't be surprised if disagreements come during this phase of building equality into your relationship. When arguments come, remember to honestly listen to each other. Also keep in mind the other rules or beliefs in the equality wheel; they will help you get through the difficult times.

Freedom to Develop Self:

Neither the power and control personality nor the victim mentality has had the freedom to develop who they really are. The power and control personality has been so busy hiding behind their insecurities and maintaining control, that they have had little energy left for self-discovery. The victim mentality has worked so hard to please and try to foresee situations that could bring trouble down on their heads, that they never considered the possibility to explore who they themselves might be.

Freedom to develop who you are is both an exhilarating experience as well as, at times, an overwhelmingly scary one. It's scary primarily because it is new. It's exhilarating because it's so exciting to finally be given permission (from both your partner and yourself) to explore your feelings, your creativity, your true likes and dislikes, your friendships, etc.

Explore and have a wonderful time! Don't forget to share all your newness with your partner. Grow together, not apart!

Laugh Together:

Laughter truly is the best cure for so many ailments. Not laughing at, but laughing together. For the (previously) power and control personality, laughter was often a tool to belittle or scoff at their partner. For the (previously) victim mentality, laughter often got them into trouble. Therefore, learning how to laugh together can take time.

Learning to laugh together can be part of the discovery of self and each other in a wonderfully healthy way. The reason laughing together is further along on the equality wheel is strategic. The other rules and/or beliefs must have firmly started to take root for laughter to become comfortable.

Being Heard:

Being heard is one of the core emotional needs we all seem to have been born with. The main reason for this seems to be that if you are not heard, you quickly assess that you don't really matter. The need to matter (or feel significant) is inborn and shapes who we become.

Reversing a life-time pattern isn't easy. It is a matter of choice!

Chapter 9
Knowing Yourself

As a counsellor, I often tell my clients that part of my job is to help them get to know themselves in every possible way.

Knowledge is power! Knowledge gives you the power to change!

What do I mean by that?

It sounds unusual to have a counsellor tell you that you need to get to know yourself. For those who have grown up in a healthy environment, getting to know yourself has been a process throughout your life. However, for those who grew up in a power and control environment, getting to know yourself is another luxury that was denied. Your very survival meant putting most of your energy into getting to know your power and control parent. This was necessary in order to avoid as much trouble as possible.

It is extremely important that you learn to listen to what your body might be saying to you. This includes your stress indicators, your anger triggers, your physically depleted indicators, your emotional needs tabulator, your healthy body vs. unhealthy body reader, as well as any number of other areas that need constant checking.

One of the best ways to get to know yourself is by doing an in-depth genogram (as mentioned in the previous chapter).

Common Genogram Symbols

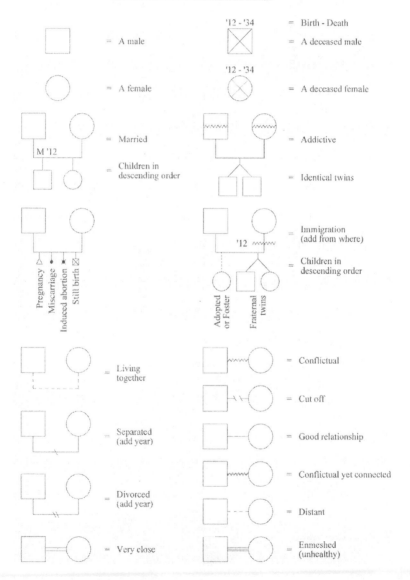

The lines and symbols can be used to trace your family history. The more detailed your personal genogram becomes, the better you will understand yourself.

You can use your genogram to keep track of each person's year of birth, the year they got married or separated or divorced, as well as whom they married, right through to the year of their death.

Your genogram can also track chronic illnesses, cause of death, country of origin, languages spoken, religion, educational background, occupation, military service, nicknames, date of retirement, trouble with the law, physical abuse, sexual abuse, incest, incest survivor, obesity, drug abuse, smoking, alcoholism, age of children leaving home, current location of family members.

Your genogram can also help you recognize how anger was dealt with, how arguments were resolved, how love was shown or not shown.

Your genogram can also help you get in touch with messages you received during your childhood years that have helped to shape your belief system. Messages regarding: self-worth, spiritual consistency, education, discipline, swearing and other forms of verbal speech, acceptable behavior, unacceptable behaviors, careers, favoritism, etc.

When we do a genogram in the counselling room, I like to help my clients see the patterns that have been developed throughout the generations of their family. I often ask them to give me a best and worst for each known member of their family. This exercise helps the client get in touch with the characteristics of each family member and often gives them an indication of where their own characteristics have come from.

The better you understand your family history, including the patterns and characteristics that have been passed down to you, the wiser your choices for your future will be able to be. The better you understand who you are, the greater your ability to break unhealthy, destructive cycles that have been passed down from one generation to the next.

Remember that knowledge of yourself and your past empowers you to take control of your own future.

About the Author

Born in Holland right after World War II, her family immigrated to Canada in the 1950s. One of twelve children, Sietske always had a thirst to learn and study.

She is a graduate of Central Baptist Seminary in Toronto, where she met her husband, John Wentworth Bellsmith. Together they were involved in missions for sixteen years, serving in the USA, Thailand, and Canada.

They have three grown children and two grandchildren, and reside in Hamilton, Ontario, Canada. They are both very active in their local church, Stanley Ave. Baptist, where Sietske is a counsellor in the Christian Counselling Centre.

She can be reached via: www.christiancounsellingcentre.com
Or via e-mail: info@christiancounsellingcentre.com